Contents

Blind justice?

How often have you seen a report about a crime in a newspaper or on TV and thought 'They should lock whoever did it up and throw away the key?' Maybe you would go one step further like this American radio show host:

66 *Turn on the juice, fry him and don't let's hear his name again.* 99
Neil Bortz, Atlanta, USA

But sometimes the punishment the person actually does get is rather a disappointment. You may think 'Is that all? No wonder there's so much crime, when criminals keep getting away with it.' Or you may think that the punishment is too severe – that the person's crime is not that bad.

Most of us are aware of crime. Some of us are worried about it, many of us are fascinated by it. We each have our own views about the punishment those who commit crime should receive, and perhaps we think we could do a better job than the police, juries and judges who are making the decisions.

66 *There are too many woolly heads running our prisons and our courts. It is time that the punishment fitted the crime.* 99
Speaker in law and order debate, British Conservative Party Conference

▼ *The goddess Justice weighs the evidence in her scales to reach a fair verdict: decisions about guilt or innocence are supposedly based on evidence alone, but other factors can help tip the balance.*

Above the Old Bailey, the Central Criminal Court in London, there is a famous statue of the goddess Justice. Justice is always considered to be blind – she does not see the accused person before her. She simply weighs the evidence of guilt and innocence in her scales and if the scales tip towards guilt the person is convicted.

In real life, of course, justice is not like this. Decisions about guilt, innocence and appropriate punishments have to be made by human beings, the judge and the jury.

66 *A jury consists of 12 persons called at random from the list of all those persons aged 18 to 70 who are registered as electors... These jurors take an oath to 'faithfully try the defendant(s) and give a true verdict according to the evidence'.* 99
The Criminal Justice System in England and Wales

But the judge and the jury *can* see the accused person before them. They can see, for instance, that the person is black, or a woman, or a drug addict, and seeing this might make a difference to the way they think. They can also hear the defendant and his or her accent may affect their view.

The jury can pause to ask why this person acted as he or she did – and take the answer into account, or not. Perhaps they heard another shocking report on the news this morning, and thought 'Crime is getting out of hand – we must do something about it.'

For these ordinary people, making difficult decisions, it is rarely just the evidence that tips the scales between guilt and innocence. All the ideas they carry in their heads about the level of crime in society, or about the way they expect certain people to behave, can play a part. And once they have decided that the accused person is guilty, these factors also play their part in deciding on a punishment that fits the crime that has been committed.

▲ Some people think you can spot criminals by the way they look or speak or by their record. The film The Usual Suspects picked up on this belief.

▼ The police arrest the suspect; the jury decides on guilt and the judge passes sentence – all play a part in finding a punishment to fit the crime.

What is crime?

What is crime? The answer might seem obvious – a crime is something such as robbery, rape or murder. It is true that throughout history and around the world there are some actions that have always been regarded as crimes, crimes that call for the severest punishment. But think about some other examples. Is taking Ecstasy a crime? Is selling alcohol? What about taking part in a religious service? Or, if you are a woman, going out in a T-shirt and shorts?

Your answers to those questions depend on where you live and the culture in which you have been brought up. Your age might also make a difference. For example, taking Ecstasy is illegal, but a young person might find it hard to think of it as a 'real' crime, despite the dangers involved:

66 *I'm not hurting anybody. I work hard during the week and at the weekend I just want to relax and forget about everything apart from having a good time.* 99 *Teenage girl, interview with author*

An older person, on the other hand, might take a very different view:

66 *You just can't afford to turn a blind eye. Before you know it they are pinching things to buy drugs and getting into all sorts of trouble. The police have got to tackle it.* 99
Elderly woman, interview with author

▲ *For women in some Muslim countries, covering up is compulsory – the penalties for showing too much flesh are severe.*

In many Islamic countries, selling alcohol is a crime – in some cases punishable by flogging! And in Iran, perhaps the most hardline of the Islamic states, women can be flogged for not covering their faces or not dressing in accordance with strict rules. Many people in Western societies find this attitude to crime very hard to understand.

◀ *'It's not a crime to enjoy yourself!' – or is it? If enjoying yourself involves the use of illegal drugs, you could end up in court charged with possession and fined. People who sell drugs face stiffer penalties.*

" As soon as I leave my room I have to put on an ankle-length mac and enveloping headscarf … I have eaten every single meal in Iran in this mac … I have stood in the midday sun sweating inside it. My mac and scarf are a very small, hot prison. "
Linda Grant, a Western tourist on holiday in Iran

If you are a member of a campaigning organization, you probably do not think twice about taking part in demonstrations or handing out leaflets. But in many parts of the world, such activities are crimes. In 1999, a British woman was sentenced to a long prison term by the Burmese government. Her crime? Singing a protest song in a public square. She was released after serving only a few weeks of her sentence, but many Burmese remain in prison for similar 'crimes'. Amnesty International, the group that campaigns for the release of political prisoners, has reported the case of five Tibetan monks sentenced to 12 to 15 years' imprisonment by the Chinese government. Their 'crime' had been to break the name plate on a government building and paste up a poster calling for independence for Tibet.

" Tens of thousands of people [in China] continued to be arbitrarily detained or imprisoned for peacefully exercising their rights to freedom of expression ... or belief. " Amnesty International, Annual Report 2003

Amnesty believes that the true number of people held for 'political crimes' is much higher than the Chinese government admits.

If crime is so hard to define, then a decision on how a crime should be punished is equally hard to reach. Punishments around the world vary as much as the definition of crime.

▼ In 1989, protestors gathered in Beijing's Tiananmen Square to call for political freedom in China. Many were killed or imprisoned when the protests were suppressed by the government.

Why commit crime?

What might make you commit a crime? If you were homeless, with no money, would you steal food? Or imagine you had a job in a bank and you had worked out a way of pocketing the takings without anyone finding out – would you do it?

The question of what makes people commit crime is a controversial one. There are probably as many answers as there are criminals. The chance to get rich quick can be as tempting for those at the top of the social ladder as for those at the bottom, though they are less likely to resort to the stocking mask and sawn-off shotgun.

▲ It is perhaps not surprising that people living on the streets are more likely to become involved in petty crime such as theft. They also run the risk of being victims of attacks and other crimes.

▼ In rundown and neglected areas, people take little or no pride in their surroundings. Vandalism, burglary and street and car crime increase, and living conditions become worse as a result.

▲ Is it greed that drives already wealthy business people to steal millions from their companies? Or is it the competitive pressure to 'get-rich-quick'?

66 Some place themselves above the law: defrauding shareholders ... and evading taxes. They are unable to comprehend that the theft of millions from ordinary taxpayers makes them into common criminals. 99 Crime and Policing, political consultation paper

There are many other possible causes of crime.

66 Unemployment, inner-city decay, drug abuse, child poverty and an ever-widening gap between the most and least prosperous in society create the conditions in which crime breeds. 99 Safer communities, safer Britain, proposals for tougher action on crime

▶ Are some people 'born criminals', as suggested in the film Natural Born Killers (far right)? Or do they, as in Bonnie and Clyde (right), just commit crime for the fun of it? And do films like these encourage violent crime by glamorizing it? These are questions to which no one has yet found a convincing answer.

For many people, it is vital to understand the circumstances in which a crime has been committed before deciding what punishment is appropriate and how to tackle crime in the future. For others, the circumstances are of little importance.

66 When I became Prime Minister I took the view that it was time to understand a little less and condemn a little more. By that I meant that we shouldn't explain away why people commit crime. We should just say bluntly 'It's wrong'. 99 John Major, former British Prime Minister, 1995

Those who share John Major's view point out that the vast majority of people living in poor social conditions do not break the law. Individuals decide to commit crime, they are not forced into it. But what about those whose behaviour is affected by psychological problems or mental illness? Child abusers, for example, have often been abused themselves as children. Is it right to understand such criminals 'a little less'? For some people, the answer would still be 'yes'.

66 Many Americans are fed up with the idea of criminals as victims. They resist and resent the argument that psychological damage relieves defendants of the responsibility for their actions. 99 US News and World Report

Going a step further, what if people are more likely to commit crime because of genetic defects, or problems at birth, or a combination of these with social factors? Research from Denmark, and other investigations into a genetic influence in crime, suggests that committing an offence might not simply be an individual's conscious decision but a result of the genetic make-up they are born with. And if that is so, how is such a person to be punished?

Does motive matter?

A teacher, who is a happily married father of two, sits calmly on a bus in Jerusalem that is taking Orthodox Jewish families home from prayers. Without warning, he activates a bomb that kills himself and 20 others, wounding 100. Six of the dead are children.

Surely everyone would agree that a terrible crime like this deserves the most serious punishment that the law allows. Yet even in a case of cold-blooded murder, the bomber believed his actions were necessary and honourable. In the incident above, the teacher was a Palestinian who considered that all Israelis must suffer for taking away his people's homeland. He was proud to be a martyr inspired by the Palestinian terrorist organisation, Hamas.

> **We are not murderers or highway-men. We are an oppressed people who have no land or home… We have maintained silence as refugees for more than 28 years.**
> Members of Black September, a Palestinian terrorist group, September 1972 (quoted in States of Terror)

There is a well-known saying that 'One man's terrorist is another man's freedom fighter'. To many Palestinians, the bomber was a hero who was fighting for a homeland for the Palestinian people.

> **The Israelis are the real criminals… They are the terrorists. Not us.** Um Ali, wife and mother of Palestinian fighters (States of Terror)

To the Israelis, however, the bomber and Hamas are criminals who forfeited their right to a fair trial. Within a week, Israelis killed a Hamas leader and four of his militants.

> **We went back to the old Biblical rule of an eye for an eye… Is it morally acceptable? One can debate that. Is it politically vital? It was.** General Aharon Yariv, former head of Israeli military intelligence (States of Terror)

If the Palestinian man had been brought to trial, should his motives

▲ The Jamaah Islamiyah terrorist group bombed two nightclubs in Bali in 2003, killing 203 people to 'avenge' Muslims oppressed by the West. Can the murder of innocent people ever be justified?

▼ Terrorist or freedom fighter? Nelson Mandela spent many years in prison for his part in the ANC's violent campaign against apartheid but is now a world figurehead.

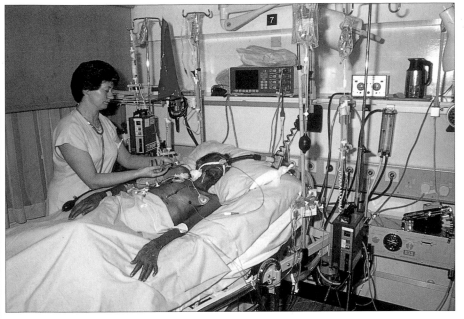

What about the motive? How much does that matter?

❝Many murders are committed under immense emotional stress by otherwise normal people who are unlikely ever to offend again: it is unnecessary to give such offenders life sentences to protect the public. Indeed, many of those convicted of murder are much less of a future danger than … persistently violent robbers. ❞ The Mandatory Life Sentence, Penal Affairs Consortium

have been taken into account? If you say 'yes', how do you deal with all the other organizations which use terror in fighting for their cause – al Qaeda in Islamic countries, ETA in Spain, guerrillas fighting Russians in Chechnya? If you say 'no', you have to be prepared for the tide of history to turn against you: Nelson Mandela and the African National Congress (ANC) were once regarded as terrorists – and not only by white South Africans – but the ANC is now in power in South Africa and Nelson Mandela is a respected world leader.

Murder can be committed for financial gain or highly idealized political ends. It can be the act of a desperate woman stabbing her partner after

years of domestic violence, or a doctor deliberately giving an overdose to a patient in pain. The end result is always the same – someone is dead. But should everyone who commits murder therefore be punished in the same way?

Judged or prejudged?

Black people make up 12 per cent of the US population, yet, in 2002, accounted for 48 per cent of prison inmates and, in 2003, over 40 per cent of people on death row. In the UK, where ethnic minorities make up just 6 per cent of the male population, approximately 19 per cent of male prisoners are from ethnic minorities. So there are far more people from ethnic minorities getting arrested and being imprisoned than you might expect, given the size of the population. Does this mean that people from

▲ *Some research suggests that ethnic minorities are treated more severely than whites by the police and courts.*

ethnic minorities are more likely to commit crimes?

The experiences of some police officers lead them to say 'yes'. In 1995 Sir Paul Condon, London's Police Commissioner (1993–2000), caused outrage when he said it was a fact that most muggings in London were carried out by young black men. Others take a very different view. Perhaps it is not that black

▼ *A video seemed to prove white police officers in Los Angeles had assaulted a black man, Rodney King. They were acquitted in 1994. Riots followed.*

people are more likely to commit crimes, but that they are more likely to be arrested.

❝ *Many police officers in metropolitan forces treat all young black men as criminals waiting to be caught.* **❞** *Marcia Hutchinson, lawyer*

Certainly, there are many black people who feel this way, and some white people share their views. The famous trial of black American football hero OJ Simpson played an important part in changing perceptions. There was uproar when it was found that a police officer closely involved with the case had boasted on previous occasions of planting evidence and beating up black suspects.

❝ *It is occurring to some white callers [to American radio shows]… that black Americans' historic distrust of the police might have been warranted all along.* **❞** *Independent on Sunday, newspaper*

After a trial lasting for nine months, the jury of ten black people and two white took just four hours to find OJ not guilty. To many, it seemed that America's black community had seized the opportunity to protect one of their own.

▲ *OJ Simpson: acquitted because he is black, or because the jury believed the evidence proved he was innocent?*

▼ *Even if this man were innocent, it might be hard to convince a jury – he fits the popular stereotype of 'the thug'.*

❝ *Suddenly OJ Simpson takes his place in the roll call of Californian verdicts that seem more about racial politics than facts or evidence … the jury had been asked to be colour-blind but had ended up blinded by colour.* **❞** *Jonathan Freedland, journalist*

There is some evidence that when people from ethnic minorities are convicted they receive longer and harsher sentences than white people. The issue is not just one of race: the verdict and sentence can also be affected by whether you are a man or a woman or by your social class. This letter from a juror gives an insight into how social prejudice can affect verdicts.

❝ *More than half the jury were obsessed with the fact that one of the defendants had tattoos, that another was black, and that they were both casually dressed and calm. From these 'facts' they deduced that these were hardened criminals.* **❞** *Guardian newspaper*

It seems that at every stage between arrest and punishment, who you are and what you look like can be as important as what you have done.

A response to public pressure?

One murder every 34 minutes, a rape every 6 minutes: the US 'crime clock' produced by the FBI indicates that the level of crime remains alarmingly high. Some of us have more cause to worry than others. In the USA, homicide is now the leading cause of death for young black males. Around the world, people in New Zealand, the USA and Australia are around six times more likely to becoming victims of violent crime than those in Switzerland, Italy and Japan.

Yet despite these figures, the actual risk of becoming a victim is still relatively low: in England and Wales, for example, only 14 per cent of recorded crimes are common assaults and in both the UK and USA crime is falling, not rising. So why do people feel so afraid? Perhaps the impression about crime given by the media plays a part.

66 The broadsheets report about three times the actual proportion of violent crime and the tabloids about ten times. The picture of the world that one gets from crime news is that it is a very violent place. Inflated perceptions of the level of violence create pressures for something to be done. 99 Roger Graef, Crime, Justice and the Media, National Association for the Care and Resettlement of Offenders (NACRO)

Does it matter if the media over-reports violent crime? They only report what they know will sell newspapers or increase a TV audience. However, imagine that you are a politician reading this newspaper column:

66 The Sun speaks its mind: Murder of children is becoming almost commonplace... Our MPs should heed the voice of the people and bring back the death penalty for child murderers... Society demands vengeance, an eye for an eye. 99 Sun newspaper

As a politician, you might know that the number of children in Britain murdered by strangers has hardly risen in forty years. But you also

◀ Over a third of people questioned in a survey were afraid to walk alone after dark. The pressure is on the forces of the law to protect us on the streets.

▲ 'Tough on crime...': Tony Blair reassures British voters in 1995 that a Labour government will not let criminals off lightly.

▲ The Republican Party in the USA promised to punish criminals more severely and believes this policy is responsible for falling crime levels.

◀ Press coverage of crime and the resulting public sympathy for the grieving families of victims leads to calls for firm action against violent crime.

know that large numbers of the people you represent read and share the newspaper's views. You are conscious that they expect you to 'do something' about crime.

Very often politicians respond to this feeling of pressure by calling for tougher sentences. When US President George W Bush, for example, signed the Protect Act of 2003 to protect children he said:

❝ This new law will formally establish the federal government's role in the Amber Alert system and will make punishment for federal crimes against children more severe. ❞ George W Bush, US President

Pressure from politicians, the public and the media eventually affects what happens in court, because judges have to take public opinion into account when they decide what sentences to impose.

❝ Sentencing today is very much driven by rhetoric concerning violent crime and our perceived inability to do anything about it. ❞
Judge Bernard Fried of the Supreme Court of the State of New York, Sentencing in the American Context, NACRO

For the prisoner in the dock, the knowledge that he or she is getting a heavier sentence than a person who committed the same crime the previous year, just because the political mood has changed, might seem like rough justice.

Are judges free to decide?

66 *A judge in a criminal court has to look an offender in the eye when imposing sentence ... the judge is inherently and individually responsible for that sentence.* 99
Judge Bernard Fried of the Supreme Court of the State of New York, Sentencing in the American Context, NACRO

Judges place great value on their freedom to decide the appropriate sentences. That does not mean, however, that judges can do whatever they like. The judge's sentence has to reflect the offence with which the person has been charged. Thus a driver who kills a child in a road accident might be charged with dangerous driving and the sentence must reflect that charge, rather than the fact that someone has died. This can be distressing for the victims and their relatives, as in this case where the driver responsible was banned from driving but received only a £250 fine.

66 *The whole process was a sham. The law did not ... censure anyone for killing my child. It found the driver guilty only of bad driving... The crash left our daughter dead and the lives of my wife and I in tatters. And that surely is not justice.* 99
Father of a crash victim

Sometimes the charge and sentence imposed are decided by 'plea bargaining'. People arrested for a serious offence plead guilty to a less serious charge, and so receive a lighter sentence. The prosecutors accept this as it avoids the risk that the jury will find the offender not guilty and that he or she will escape punishment all together. Plea bargaining saves time and money, and it is a very important feature of the US system. It does mean, however, that many people are not receiving the punishment that really fits their crime.

Even judges are sometimes told what sentence they can impose.

▶ *In some European countries, a driver who kills can face manslaughter charges; the judge can take account of the fact that someone has died when deciding the sentence.*

▼ *The judge's gavel and block symbolize his or her authority. But do judges really have the last say?*

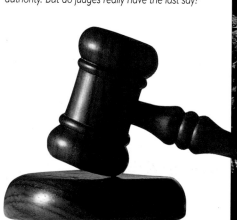

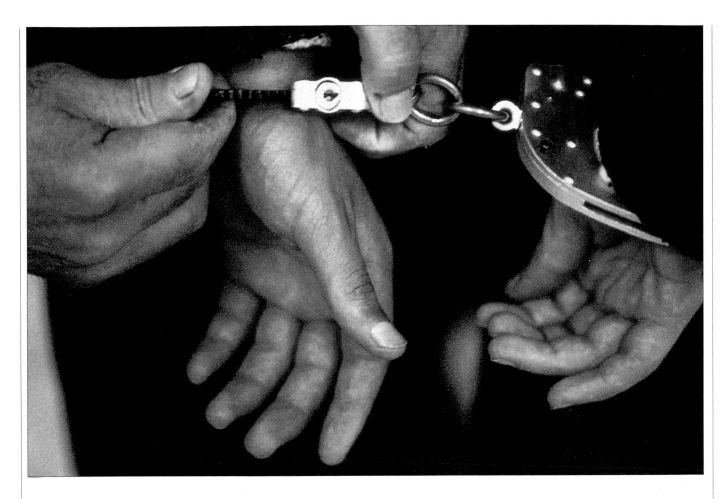

European law, for example, often has power over national courts, as in human rights cases. Also, in the UK, convicted murderers must receive life imprisonment. Many people who work in the legal system find the mandatory life sentence very frustrating, as it prevents the judge from taking account of the many different circumstances in which this crime might be committed.

❝ *It is fundamentally wrong in principle that a judge should be required to pass upon the wife who has been maltreated for years by a brutal husband, and eventually kills him, precisely the same sentence as … upon the ruthless shotgun robber.* **❞** *Committee on the Penalty for Homicide*

▲ *There is a long way between making an arrest and passing sentence. Judges, like prisoners, can sometimes find that their hands are tied.*

▶ *Sara Thornton claimed that years of abuse drove her to kill her husband. She received a life sentence for murder but was eventually released.*

In the USA, the introduction of 'three-strikes' laws, in which a person convicted of three violent crimes must serve a life sentence, and tighter controls on sentencing have further reduced the freedom of individual judges to decide on appropriate punishment. If the process continues, many feel it will become ever harder for the judge to look the prisoner in the eye and be confident that the sentence he or she is passing is a just one.

Protecting society?

Punishment is not just about making sure a criminal gets his or her 'just deserts'. Lawmakers also have to consider how to protect society from crime in the future. Argument focuses on the best way to do this.

Research into patterns of crime shows that a relatively small proportion of people commit a large proportion of crimes. One factor in deciding how to punish them is the need to keep them 'off the streets' for as long as possible.

> 66 *Researchers have looked at a sample of burglars who had been given a community sentence. They found that if they had gone to prison instead, this would have prevented between 3 and 13 crimes. Per burglar. Per year.* 99 Michael Howard, former British Home Secretary, 1994

The idea of locking people up to protect the rest of society from them – a theory known as 'incapacitation' – is more popular in some countries than others. Britain, for example, imprisons more people than any other country in Western Europe. In some countries, 'incapacitation' is taken to extremes – in Saudi Arabia and Iran thieves have their hands amputated, making it physically more difficult for them to reoffend. The ultimate form of incapacitation is the death penalty, removing the

▲ *Safe behind bars? Sending more people to prison, and keeping them inside for longer, is one way of tackling crime.*

criminal for ever.

The death penalty is also seen by some as the ultimate deterrent but deterrence can take all sorts of other, less final, forms. Fining parents for their children's bad behaviour is supposed to deter them from allowing their offspring to run wild in future. Physical punishments such as caning, are practised in various countries, such as Singapore. The reintroduction of the chain gang in the US state of Alabama is designed to make prison so unpleasant that no one will ever want to experience it again. Humiliating punishments can also be seen as having a deterrent effect.

▼ *A demonstration of caning in a Singapore prison. Some people view caning as an effective deterrent; others see it as a human rights abuse.*

> **❝** *I think that the most effective way of dealing with people who steal from shops, knock old people down and commit vandalism is simply to put them in the stocks … and let them come face to face with the public they have injured.* **❞** _Contributor to radio phone-in programme_

The underlying aim of both deterrence and incapacitation is to protect the public and prevent reoffending. Punishments that emphasize rehabilitation are a different means to the same end. Rehabilitative punishment focuses on tackling the behaviour or the circumstances that led an offender into crime in the first place – for example, by tackling drug addiction or providing therapy for sex offenders.

As in most aspects of life, however, fashions in punishment change. In many Western societies, rehabilitation is now seen as a 'soft option'.

> **❝** *It cannot be denied that 'the people' call for a more severe approach to crime … perhaps they believe that only severe punishment provides the necessary deterrence to procure safety and peace for themselves…* **❞**
> _Judge Willem Van Schendel of Amsterdam's Court of Appeal, No Silence in Court, NACRO_

▶ *Exhaustion after a day's hard labour in the chain gang (top); humiliation in the stocks (middle); developing self-respect by earning money from painting (right) – which is the best way to prevent people reoffending?*

A life for a life?

❝*In New York, the death penalty has turned the tables on fear and put it back where it belongs – in the hearts of the criminals. Within just one year, the death penalty helped produce a dramatic drop in violent crime. I know, as do most New Yorkers, that by restoring the death penalty, we have saved lives.***❞*** New York Governor George Pataki*

The worldwide trend is towards abolition of the death penalty, but with the strong statement above in mind, it is perhaps not surprising that the USA has turned to capital punishment as the ultimate weapon in its fight against crime. As far as its supporters are concerned, the death penalty is the only punishment appropriate to the taking of a life.

❝*For the rules to be obeyed, they must be accompanied by a sanction that fits the crime… [The death penalty] is a legitimate expression of moral indignation, a notice that certain acts are simply unacceptable…***❞**
Gary L McDowell, Director (1992–2003), Institute of US Studies and Professor of American Studies, University of London

▶ *In the USA, the death penalty can be carried out by hanging, lethal injection, firing squad, gassing or electrocution in an 'electric chair' (shown right). None of these methods is painless.*

Not everyone who supports the use of the death penalty suggests that it should be used for all murders. The Police Federation in the UK, for example, supports its use for premeditated murder. Others think it should be used for those who kill police officers, or for child murderers, or terrorists.

For those who oppose the death penalty, none of the above views cut much ice. To some, its use is simply immoral and brings the law down to the level of the criminal.

66 *With each person excuted, we're teaching our children that the way to settle scores is through violence, even to the point of taking a human life* 99 *Russ Feingold, US Senator*

Awareness that the legal system treats some people more harshly than others can also make the death penalty intolerable.

66 *Death sentences in the USA are handed out disproportionately against the poor and members of ethnic minority groups...* 99 *Amnesty International Report, 1999*

In the UK in the early 1990s many people's faith in the legal system was shaken when it was discovered that several men and women gaoled for a series of IRA bombings twenty years earlier were innocent; those people would almost certainly have been hanged had the UK not abolished capital punishment in 1969.

▶ *The Birmingham Six were wrongly convicted of IRA bombings. They might have been executed if Britain had retained capital punishment.*

Despite this, those in favour of the death penalty argue that it acts as a deterrent. However, there is not much evidence to support this: murder rates in countries which use the death penalty carry on rising. A survey of police chiefs in the USA found that two-thirds did not believe it had any deterrent effect, partly because so few people actually think about the consequences of a crime before committing it. Their view is

▼ *Many believe child killers like the notorious Moors murderer, Ian Brady, should face the death penalty for their crimes.*

shared by Albert Pierrepoint, Britain's hangman for 25 years:

66 *I do not believe that any one of the hundreds of executions I carried out has in any way acted as a deterrent against future murder. Capital punishment in my view achieved nothing except revenge.* 99 *Albert Pierrepoint, quoted by Amnesty International*

▼ *A lynch mob kills a suspected criminal illegally without trial. Does the death penalty simply legalize this kind of mob-rule justice?*

What is the point of prison?

In Western societies which do not use the death penalty, prison is the toughest form of punishment that a criminal can receive.

❝Last year I said something controversial. I said 'Prison works'.❞ Michael Howard, former British Home Secretary, 1994

By 'works', Michael Howard implied three things: firstly, prison takes criminals off the street, secondly, it punishes them for their crimes and, thirdly, it stops them reoffending. Prison populations in Britain rose rapidly, increasing by almost a third in four years, as the 'Prison works' idea filtered through the system. By 1999, there were 66,000 held in prisons in the UK. A similar situation occurred in the USA.

❝If [America's] prison population continues to grow at the same staggering rate, experts predict there will soon be more US citizens in prison than there are full-time college students.❞
Guardian newspaper

In theory, the 'punishment' in being sent to prison lies in the fact that the criminal has been deprived of his or her freedom. In practice, conditions in prisons often result in an extra element of punishment. In

What is the point of prison? What should living conditions be like in prison? Most prisons in the developed world (top) are supposed to be 'decent but austere'. Poorer countries like Bolivia (centre) perhaps cannot afford to make life comfortable for prisoners but sometimes miserable conditions are part of the punishment (bottom).

Russia, for example, a team of UN investigators found prisoners being held in dirty conditions which were causing the spread of disease: beds had to be shared, with inmates sleeping in shifts, and food was poor.

Often, poor conditions are the result of overcrowding, inadequate sanitation in old buildings and a lack of money to tackle the problem. Sometimes, it is deliberate policy to hold prisoners in harsh conditions.

66 *Here at the Maine Correctional Institute, also known as the Super Max, we are locked in solitary confinement for 23 hours a day. Most of us are not permitted to go outside for recreation, receive no fresh air.* 99 *Letter from prison inmate, printed in newsletter of Coalition for Prisoners' Rights*

However, prisoners rarely stay inside for ever. As a report into the UK prison system pointed out:

66 *The Prison Service has to live… with prisoners during their time in prison. The rest of the country lives with them afterwards.* 99
Woolf Report, 1991

Many feel that prison should put more emphasis on training and treatment rather than punishment.

66 *On the Sex Offender Treatment Programme, we are given skills and knowledge to understand why we offend… We learn how to identify and practise methods of avoiding offending again.* 99 *Convicted sex offender in a UK prison, quoted in the magazine Prison Report*

This sort of approach may enable prisoners to leave better equipped to deal with life on the outside.

Faced with rising numbers of prisoners, those who actually have to run prisons have called for the importance of rehabilitation to be remembered.

66 *We believe that imprisonment is the punishment and that regimes should be based upon a rehabilitative approach… It is after all the only way in which prison can work.* 99 *Manifesto for Change, Prison Governors' Association, UK*

But many people are unhappy with a prison system that can sometimes appear to reward offenders while ignoring the plight of their victims.

▲ *Rooms inside a women's prison can be comfortable. An inmate's loss of personal freedom is seen as punishment enough.*

▼ *Inmates are often given work in prison. This may help prepare them to find work after leaving.*

Getting tough: a deterrent?

Young people account for between one-third and a half of all arrests and convictions in the USA and UK. The vast majority are young men, and many are well known to the courts, as they persistently reoffend. These young people, like everyone else, have been affected by the move to 'get tough' on crime.

I set out to turn the tide on crime… We shall shortly be opening two tough new prison regimes … to shock young offenders out of drifting into crime. John Major, former British Prime Minister, 1995

The type of prison John Major referred to is commonly known as a 'boot camp'. There are now around 50 camps in 34 states in the USA and other countries are considering introducing them. They are designed to deter young people from reoffending by putting them through a fairly short but tough regime of military-style physical training and work. A boot-camp sentence is

▲ Military-style training is meant to encourage self-discipline. But is it appropriate to train a young offender to be a soldier?

usually given to young men, aged 16-25, convicted of non-violent offences. Is it appropriate to treat young offenders in this way? Yes, say some.

I'm grateful to the judge for sentencing me to boot camp. It's given me a chance to sort my life out. Inmate of an American boot camp, speaking on a radio programme

Others are less convinced, believing it may even encourage violence.

A model which was designed to train and prepare men for war is not an appropriate method for deterring and rehabilitating young offenders. New South Wales Department of Corrective Services, Australia, 1991, quoted in Boot Camps: Return of the Short, Sharp Shock, The Prison Reform Trust

A young man who underwent the 'short sharp shock' treatment, which Britain introduced in the early 1980s and was similar to boot camps, described his experience of them in this way.

I was angry because I suffered physical and verbal abuse by other inmates … and by prison officers. Needless to say I carried on offending … but in a much more aggressive way, i.e. mindless vandalism. Chip on my shoulder? Dead right. Letter to the Guardian newspaper

▼ The treatment of young offenders has been influenced by concerns over the rise of violent crime.

24

▲ Boot camp inmates are shouted at constantly. Even the guards can find the role of 'sergeant major' stressful and demoralizing.

▲ Shaved heads, early starts and plenty of hard work are all part of the boot-camp experience.

So the important question is do boot camps work? Do they deter convicted criminals from reoffending? Those who were keen to introduce the camps in Britain believed that they do. With a change of government in Britain, enthusiasm for boot camps waned and the tough regimes were not extended to other prisons. In the USA, it is the boot camps which put most emphasis on education and training that have had the greatest success in stopping reoffending and past UK experience is not encouraging:

❝ In 1979, the then Home Secretary, William Whitelaw, delighted the Conservative Party Conference when he promised detention centres where young criminals would get a 'short, sharp, shock'… Five years later a Home Office report found the regime had had no discernible effect on reconviction. It was made tougher but still had no noticeable effect. The short, sharp shock was quietly shelved… ❞ John McLeod, journalist

Rehabilitation: a soft option?

The aim of rehabilitation is to help offenders to lead 'law-abiding and useful lives' in the community. Some prison regimes offer education and training to help people when they are released and rehabilitation is also an important element in alternative forms of punishment, such as community service or probation. Sentences like these can bring benefits to the whole community, not just to the offenders themselves.

66 *We have a lovely time when we come here and the young people are so helpful, it's hard to think that they have been in trouble.* **99**
74-year-old member of lunch club run by community service unit quoted in Paying Back: Twenty Years of Community Service

There are concerns, however, that the alternatives to prison are hardly punishments at all, and that, as a result criminals are being allowed to 'get away with it'. This can cause resentment.

66 *Punishment in the community can be a real alternative. But it must be a deterrent. It must involve real work – and not be a soft option.* **99** *John Major, former British Prime Minister*

However, many of those who work with young offenders believe that

community service only succeeds when offenders are given work that is of real value. Long hours doing tedious, unskilled jobs do not help to prevent reoffending – some feel they may even encourage it.

66 *The overall aim is that having been given a sense of achievement, possibly having learned or improved skills … the offender will be less likely to reoffend and more likely to have found constructive ways of occupying free time.* **99**
Probation officer quoted in Paying Back: Twenty Years of Community Service

▲ *Helping the community: under supervision a trusted prisoner spends time with a young visitor.*

Does community service work? Some people have their doubts.

66 *The latest research shows that there is little difference between the reconviction rates of those sent to prison and those given community service or probation orders. Given that the most hardened criminals are sent to prison, it is perhaps surprising that the differences are not greater.* **99** *Law and Order, Politics Today, Conservative Party Research Department*

Research like this has encouraged people to turn once more to imprisonment. However, the key to improving the success of rehabilitative programmes might be in an even more radical approach. A scheme for persistent young offenders is being tested in the UK. It combines close supervision by the police with education and a programme of help with social problems.

66 *If they want de-tox [treatment for drug or alcohol addiction], there wouldn't be a waiting list for them to get into a centre. With housing they would go to the top of the list. For employment and training, packages would be offered… Unless we address those social problems they are going to continue offending. It's not rewarding crime.* 99
Mary Geaney, Youth Justice official

Not everyone will be convinced that this is not a reward for crime.

But those who support rehabilitation programmes, just like the people who support boot camps, or the death penalty, are all trying to find answers to difficult questions – not only 'Does the punishment fit the crime?' but also 'What works'?'.

▲ *As an alternative to prison some offenders work on 'team building' community programs, such as this one in Connecticut, USA.*

▼ *Giving young offenders their own home, helping them find work – some people think this is the best way to help prevent them reoffending.*

Cost-effective justice?

Solving crime, bringing criminals to justice and administering the punishment all have to be paid for. Before taking a suspect to court, the police and prosecuters must decide whether they have a good case – many people view a not-guilty verdict as a waste of court time and tax-payers' money so cases frequently never make it to trial. The pressure to achieve convictions has also led to the development of plea bargaining (see page 16).

In the case of punishment, sometimes costs seem to outweigh the level of the crime. Recently more people, particularly women, have been sent to prison for unpaid debts.

▼ Crime costs everyone money: millions of pounds have to be spent on the police, courts and prison services.

▲ As prison populations rise, money has to be spent on new prisons and maintaining old ones. It cost £5,000,000 to refurbish this UK prison.

❝Geri Andrews was fined £400 for non-payment of a £15 parking ticket and failure to display a £140 car tax disc. She couldn't pay the fine and was imprisoned for 14 days. Her two children were taken into care. Her punishment is likely to have cost the state in the region of £4000. ❞
Report of a UK court case

However, crime at whatever level needs to be punished and the cost has to be balanced against the effectiveness of the punishment – in protecting the public and reducing reoffending. Recent research shows that increasing the number of people sent to prison by 25 per cent only reduces the level of crime by around 1 per cent.

66 The decision needs to be made about whether the costs of increasing the prison population… are worth paying to achieve a reduction of this order in crime. 99 What works in dealing with crime?, NACRO

It costs around £2,500 per month to keep a prisoner in gaol. By contrast community service and probation orders cost about £200 per month to carry out. There seems to be little to choose between them in terms of preventing people reoffending. If you believe that prison works, you might think that the extra cost is well worth paying. If you do not, perhaps you agree with the view that:

66 Prison can be an expensive way of making bad people worse. 99 Crime, Justice and Protecting the Public, UK government report

Cost is an important factor in developing new approaches to punishment. Part of the appeal of boot camps is that offenders should be in there for a 'short, sharp shock', rather than for a long and more expensive sentence.

Perhaps the best way to tackle crime is to spend far more on crime prevention. Of all the crimes committed no more than half are reported to the police and of these there are convictions in only 3 per cent of cases.

66 Deterrence, incapacitation and rehabilitation depend upon there being an individual on whom they might have an effect. 99 What works in dealing with crime?, NACRO

Until crime prevention becomes more effective, efforts must go on to find punishments that reflect the seriousness of the crime; that are fair to the offender; that are not distorted by popular pressure and ensure that the offender has no more victims. Only when this is achieved will we truly have found a punishment that fits the crime.

▲ *Spending more on crime prevention schemes such as Neighbourhood Watch might be a more cost-effective way of tackling crime.*

▼ *The 'Guardian Angel' volunteers patrol the streets like a police force. Some feel that this type of group is the wrong sort of crime prevention as it may take the law into its own hands.*

Glossary

ANC: African National Congress, an organization that fought for the rights of the black majority in South Africa and is now in power there.

BROADSHEET: A newspaper printed on large sheets of paper – it usually means a more 'serious' newspaper.

CAPITAL PUNISHMENT: The punishment by which a person found guilty is sentenced to death for his crimes.

CENSURE: To criticize severely; governments will sometimes blame or censure a person or organization for a particular occurrence.

COUNSEL: Advice; counsel is often used to describe the barrister or solicitor working on a case.

DEDUCED: Reached an opinion or solution from events that have occurred or information provided.

DEFENDANT: The person who has been accused of committing a crime and is being tried for it.

DE-TOX: An abbreviation for detoxification, the treatment to cure drug or alcohol addiction.

DETERRENT: Something that prevents an event from happening; a punishment that aims to put people off committing crime in future.

FBI: Federal Bureau of Investigation, an agency that investigates crimes in the USA.

GENETIC: Relating to genes, elements that are passed from parent to child which control some aspects of appearance and behaviour.

HOMICIDE: The killing of one person by another.

IRA: Irish Republican Army, an organization that fights for an end to British rule in Northern Ireland. Members of the IRA are generally viewed as terrorists.

JURY: Group of people who attend a trial and have to decide whether the defendant is guilty, on the basis of the evidence presented to them.

MANSLAUGHTER: The act of killing someone unlawfully but not intentionally.

MILITIA: A group of people enrolled and drilled as soldiers; 'unofficial' militia are often the basis for terrorist organizations.

MURDER: The act of killing someone unlawfully and intentionally.

PAROLE: The process by which prisoners are released before the end of the sentence.

PREMEDITATED: Planned in advance.

PROBATION: The system by which offenders are placed under the supervision of a probation officer and perhaps requiring them to undertake treatment or training, or to live in a certain place.

PROCURE: To obtain or acquire.

RAPE: The act of forcing someone to have sexual intercourse against his or her will.

REGIME: A system of government or management.

REHABILITATION: The process of helping someone to fit better into society, through training, treatment, etc.

SANCTION: A specific penalty or punishment attached to a crime.

SOLITARY CONFINEMENT: The punishment of keeping a prisoner locked up alone.

TABLOID: A newspaper printed on small pages – usually used of a newspaper that carries many human interest stories, sex scandals, etc.

WARRANTED: Justified, correct.

Useful Addresses

UK

Amnesty International UK
99–119 Rosebery Avenue
London EC1R 4RE
Tel: 020 7814 6200
www.amnesty.org.uk

Research, Development and
Statistics Directorate (RDS)
Room 811, Home Office
50 Queen Anne's Gate
London SW1H 9AT
Tel: 020 7273 2084
www.homeoffice.gov.uk/rds

NACRO (National Association for the
Care and Resettlement of Offenders)
169 Clapham Road
London SW9 0PU
Tel: 020 7582 6500
www.nacro.org.uk

Victim Support
Cranmer House
39 Brixton Road
London SW9 6DZ
Tel: 020 7735 9166
www.victimsupport.org.uk

Prison Reform Trust
15 Northburgh Street
London EC1V 0JR
www.prisonreformtrust.org.uk

Australia

New South Wales Department
of Corrective Services
Roden Cutler House
24 Campbell Street
Sydney NSW 2000
www.dcs.nsw.gov.au

Facts to think about

◆ Surveys show that people think about half of all crime is violent crime but in England and Wales 77 per cent of recorded crimes are against property.

◆ In 2002 in the USA, there were 1,309 male prisoners per 100,000 men, compared with 113 female prisoners per 100,000 women.

◆ People from ethnic minorities are over-represented in the prison population – in the UK men from ethnic minorities make up just 6 per cent of the population, but 19 per cent of sentenced prisoners.

◆ Over 80 per cent of crimes are committed by men.

◆ Surveys suggest that only half of crimes committed are actually reported to the police and just 2 per cent result in a conviction.

◆ Crime has been falling in the USA since 1992. In 2002, crimes of violence and against property reached their lowest level for 30 years.

◆ The peak age for offending is 18 for men and 15 for women.

◆ A survey carried out in five British cities showed that 61 per cent of all those arrested had traces of drugs in their bodies. Cannabis was the most common, with 10 per cent testing positive for cocaine and crack.

◆ Almost half the countries in the world no longer use the death penalty. Over half of all the death penalties carried out each year take place in China.

◆ Since 1990, Amnesty International has documented 33 executions of child offenders in seven countries. Eighteen of these were in the USA.

◆ 'Life' sentences are given for murder and other serious crimes – although most 'lifers' will only spend 12-16 years inside.

◆ During 2002–03 in England and Wales, a person had a 27 per cent chance of becoming a victim of crime, compared with 40 per cent in 1995.

Index